I Was There:

Dramatic Monologues
For
Christmas Transformation

by David Inglis

DEDICATION:

To Carolyn, Emily, and Dan, my beloved family and to the Henrietta UCC, my loving family of faith.

I WAS THERE: Dramatic Monologues for Christmas Transformation

by David Inglis

ISBN 1-57438-027-3

Educational Ministries, Inc.
165 Plaza Drive
Prescott, AZ 86303
800-221-0910

Contents

Joseph

"The Impossible Dream"

Matthew 1:18-25

Do you believe in dreams? I mean, if you had a dream that flew in the face of all logic and all the evidence, how long would it take you to stop believing the dream and start believing your eyes and your brain?

I had a dream about an angel one night long, long ago that I wanted with all my heart to believe. If I could be sure that that dream were true, I knew that I could face all the trouble I was in without buckling under.

I guess you know the kind of trouble I was in, too. Mary and I were betrothed. You don't have anything quite like our betrothals here in your country. It was more than being engaged: it was a binding commitment that could only be ended by divorce. But when you were betrothed, you didn't live together and there was no physical intimacy. So there we were, just betrothed, but Mary was looking more and more pregnant every week and I hadn't done anything. I had never been so hurt, and embarrassed, and confused in all my life.

As a matter of fact, I have always taken great pains to never let myself get into a compromising situation. I have always been a righteous man.

I always believed that God is a just God. He smiles on those who obey Him with His blessings. And it seemed like God had been smiling on me. People respected my carpentry work and gave me enough business to buy the necessities of life. I had good friends. And God gave me Mary as my future wife. Mary had the most beautiful smile, and eyes that danced with life. Mary had a heart of gold. And I knew that Mary loved and respected me. I just thanked God every night for giving me such a wonderful young woman to be my wife.

But then, for reasons I couldn't explain, it seemed like God's smile on me turned into a frown. Everything started to go wrong, very wrong. Mary was pregnant. She pleaded with me to believe her—that an angel had told her that God's Spirit had conceived this child, and he would be called the Son of God. Now what would you think if someone gave you an explanation like that of why she was pregnant? I have always been a man of reason. I don't let myself get carried away with strange ideas. Mary seemed so sincere as she begged me to believe her, and so desperate. I wanted to believe it, and to believe that I was the only one for her. But you can't base your decisions on wishes, and displays of emotion, and stories of angels.

The night that Mary told me she was pregnant, God had never seemed so far away. My dreams, my heart, my faith, were all crushed into a thousand broken pieces that night. I ran out into the night and saw the stars spread out above me like a huge canopy. "God! What are You doing to me? I thought I was following Your law and Your holy will. I thought Mary was Your gift to me! Why is this happening to me?" And do you know what answer I got back? Dead silence. NOTHING. The sky was EMPTY, and I was alone. It's hard for me to admit this to you, even now, but I thought about doing a horrible thing. I thought about tying a rope around my neck, and jumping out of a tree, and joining the emptiness of the vast darkness out there. Wouldn't that be better than my pain?

But our law strictly forbids taking your own life. Our law seemed to know of despair and loss of faith. But could the law hold me accountable if the Giver of the Law, God Himself, was unjust, or deaf, or gone?

I didn't know if the law was worth anything any more. But I had nothing else to go by, so I clung to it like an anchor in a storm. The law gave me two choices for how to handle an unfaithful woman. I could publicly take her to court, expose her as an adulteress, and watch her be sentenced to stoning. Oh, I could not do that to my Mary, no matter what she had done. Or I could give her papers of divorce in the presence of two witnesses. That's what I would do. I would find two people I could trust to keep things as quiet as possible.

It was while I was considering who would make the best witnesses that I had my strange dream. A being, glowing with brightness, stood over my bed and called: "Joseph, do not be afraid to take Mary home as your wife, because what is conceived in her is from the Holy Spirit. She will give birth to a son, and you are to give him the name Jesus, which means `the Lord saves,' because he will save his people from their sins."

When I woke up, that dream was still very vivid in my mind. But did I dare to believe it? Was it really God talking to me, or was it my wishes taking control of my imagination?

Something made me think back to words spoken long ago by the prophet Isaiah to King Ahaz, who had lost his faith in the face of his enemies who were plotting his downfall. Isaiah said, "The Lord himself will give you a sign: The virgin will be with child and will give birth to a son, and will call him Emmanuel." Isaiah's message was that even in the midst of Ahaz's darkness and despair, God would make Himself known in the birth of a child, and his name, Emmanuel, would be a reminder of God's presence. Emmanuel means "God is with us."

Could God be with me, even when life had plunged me into darkness? Could I dare to believe in a sign that no one else could see, and I couldn't prove even to myself?

You probably never realized how hard it was for me to really believe what I wished so much might be true. I knew that if I believed that dream enough to act on it, I would face the ridicule of my people. And I was right. When I didn't divorce Mary, of course everyone assumed that I had gotten her pregnant, and my reputation as an honest, law-abiding man was erased in one stroke. Business really dropped off. I could no longer say that God was making sure I got what I needed to live on.

I tried to explain my dream about the angel to a few trusted friends. "Dreams," they said to me. "Everyone has dreams, Joseph. If you had only divorced Mary like the law says, you could have started over and at least kept your reputation." Then they shook their heads, "But it's too late for that now."

My friends were no help. So I tried to explain everything to the rabbi. "Joseph," he said. "I have never known anyone in our time to receive a message from God in this way, though I have known some who would like us to think they have. But Joseph, I know you are an honest man. If this is of God, He will show you that He is with you. You can be sure of that; He will show you."

The rabbi's words seemed wise and true. But those words churned up doubt and worry when I heard Caesar's decree that I had to go to Bethlehem to enroll for the tax, just when Mary was almost ready to deliver. Mary and I had no one in the world now but each other and our dreams of angels. We just had to be together, surely God knew that. But now God seemed to be frowning on us again: we had to travel to Bethlehem. "If this is of God, He will show you that He is with you," the rabbi had said. Was God with us?

The rabbi's words churned up frustration and anger as we made that long, hard journey from Nazareth to Bethlehem with Mary bone weary and hurting with every jostle, and the donkey stubborn and ornery, and night winds that blew through our garments like they were fish nets. "If this is of God, He will show you that He is with you." Was God with us?

The rabbi's words swept me with a feeling of helpless loneliness as I desperately searched Bethlehem for a bed where Mary could deliver our homeless baby. "If this is of God, He will show you that He is with you." WAS GOD WITH US, when all I could find was a dung-splattered stable hollowed out of a cave, with skittish animals threatening to trample Mary and the helpless baby in the dark?

What had become of my dream, that this child was conceived by God's Spirit and was God's special child? How long would *you* hang onto a promise, a hope, your faith, when everything you saw and everything your mind told you flew in the face of it? How long?

I looked over at Mary, who was nursing the baby and trying to keep it warm. What if we couldn't find enough for Mary to eat to produce milk? What if it got too cold for the clothes we had with us to keep the baby warm? I felt like a terrible provider. If God was the father of the child, He sure wasn't doing much of a job providing for His Son either. The candle's flame caught Mary's eyes as she looked towards me. Those eyes that used to dance with life were flowing with tears. We were two good law-abiding people whose lives and dreams had been shattered. Why? Was God mocking us, or just gone?

I should have given the baby his name by now. "Jesus" was what the angel had told me to name him: "the Lord saves." "The Lord saves"? How could I name him that, after all that had happened?

When Mary set the baby into the manger, he began to cry. He knew this place was barely fit for an animal. But then, above the crying, we heard footsteps and voices outside. My heart started racing, my fists were clenched.

A shepherd's face appeared in the candlelight, rough and weatherbeaten, but with such a look of innocent wonder in his eyes that my hands relaxed right away. "Is there a baby in here?" he asked. The baby's crying gave him his answer. "Here he is!" he shouted to the other men who were with him.

"Here who is? This is our baby," I said.

"Well, I suppose that's right," the first shepherd said. "Of course he's yours. But an angel just told us he's born to us too, to be our savior, the Messiah."

"An angel told you that?" All the shepherds sheepishly nodded their heads. "Yeah, can you believe an angel talking to us? And not only one angel, we saw a whole bunch of angels, and we heard them singing too! I know it sounds crazy, but we all saw it just the same way. Can we see the baby, please?"

They all spilled into the stable like an excited bunch of young boys. They knelt down in front of that tiny baby of ours in that cold cave, and thanked God and prayed like they were in a holy place. As I watched those rough-hewn shepherds, the rabbi's words came back to me one more time. "If this is of God, He will show you that He is with you, you can be sure of that. He will show you."

I sat down beside Mary and grasped her trembling hand. What did all of this mean? Could this helpless baby, born into a dark and cold stable so far from home, born to a couple whose faith had been shaken to the core, born to a people who lived under the power of pagan Rome, could this tiny baby be God's own Son, the Messiah, the Savior? Was God coming to us as a fragile human being, to be *with us* in our darkness and our suffering, and show us the way somehow to the light?

I got on my knees and took my place next to the shepherds as we looked at this little baby, now sleeping peacefully in the manger.

"What's his name?" one of them whispered.

"His name is Jesus," I told him. "It means, 'The Lord saves.' "

Mary

"Let It Be"

Luke 1:26-45

Everybody knows who I am. I'm Mary, the mother of Jesus. But do you *really* know who I am? Am I the pure, unspotted virgin, all meek and mild? Am I the Holy Mother that people can pray to if they have a hard time approaching the stern Father on His heavenly throne? Am I like a passionless pastel statue, who never doubted or feared or cried?

Who am I, really? I think you can come to know me best by looking into your *own* life, and recalling the times when you felt overwhelmed, confused, and afraid. At least that's where you have to begin, if you really want to know me.

I was only a teenager when my simple life was turned upside down by the visit from the angel Gabriel. In my young heart, I had felt a longing to serve God in any way He showed me. But I *never* expected that an actual angel would appear to *me*. And I never, *ever* would have imagined that I would have been chosen to be the mother of such an important child!

It would have been much easier if I had been hoping and praying for a child, like my elderly cousin Elizabeth. I would have blushed with humility, and then felt a joyful pride welling up inside, to think that I had been chosen for such an honor. But I can't describe the turmoil that churned up in me when

Gabriel told me I was going to bear God's special child before I was even married. How could my desire to serve God and do what was right have led me into something that seemed so...bizarre, so wrong?

I stood there speechless, trying to make some sense out of the angel's disturbing words that I would bear the Son of the Most High. "How can this happen?" I finally stammered. "I am a virgin!" If *anybody* knew that, I certainly expected God to!

Gabriel seemed to understand my confusion. "The Holy Spirit will come upon you, and the power of the Most High will cover you. The baby will be holy. He will be called the Son of God." What I got from this angel talk was that God was going to do something that had never happened before, and that this child wouldn't be an ordinary human being. But what I *couldn't* understand was how people were going to believe that the baby was God's son, instead of believing that I was a sinful girl. I mean, I could scarcely believe that this was really happening myself.

Gabriel seemed to be waiting for my answer, but I felt no impatience or pressure from him. I had prayed to be shown God's will for my life. But what God was asking of me was going to be hard. Very hard. Why did God have to choose me?

And what about Joseph? I had dreamed of what it would be like being his wife, and supporting him as he started his own carpentry shop. What would happen to those dreams now? Could Joseph ever believe me? The righteous people would never bring their business to him now, if they thought there was sin in the family. Maybe I could politely decline this "honor," live a righteous life, and still pursue my own dreams. But could I ever be satisfied with my life, knowing I had refused to do what God had asked of me?

I took a deep breath and told the angel, "I am the servant of the Lord. Let it be with me according to your word."

"Let it be with me according to your word." With that assent, I let go of all my plans, my hopes, my dreams. I tried to look into the future, hoping Gabriel or God or someone would tell me what was in store for me now. But the angel was gone. I was staring into the darkness of the unknown, alone.

That night, I had a vivid dream that I was so close to God, I could feel Him filling every part of my body, mind, and spirit with powerful light and love. It was like being bathed, or flooded...I can't find any words that can describe how glorious it was. It was like being in the highest heaven. When I woke up, I felt like I was glowing from the inside out with this heavenly power. I hummed and sang to myself as I set about my earthly duties of cleaning, cooking and fetching water. But I kept thinking about the new life I was sure I was carrying inside me now. What would happen when it started to grow, and I started to show? I knew it was God's baby, and somehow everything would be all right. I *had* to trust that. But I sure needed someone to talk to. I needed someone who I knew would stand by me no matter what. I needed to tell my mother.

When I tried to explain it all to her, worry seized her face. "Oh, my poor Mary!"

She put my head in her lap, felt my forehead, and stroked my hair like she did when I was sick with a fever. "What's happening to my poor child? I always knew you were too sensitive. Mary, everybody has strange dreams now and then. You can't believe everything that pops into your imagination. I think I've been making you work too hard. Please, just rest today, and tomorrow too. I'm sure you'll feel better soon."

"But Mama, I'm not sick! How can I make you believe this is *real*?" I stood up right in front of her. My heart sank as I saw the look of fear on her face. "You know Rachael, Jethro's wife?" she asked. "When she was about your age, she was given to terrible dreams, and seeing spirits too, she said. People thought she was possessed. It went on for close to a year. But she came out of it, and now she's got two fine children. Please, Mary, don't talk about this any more. Not another word! *Do you hear me, child*?"

"Yes, Mama," and I quickly walked outside and released a flood of lonely tears. I had to talk to Joseph. He needed to know what was happening. Maybe Gabriel had told him too.

In the heat of the day, when most everyone was off the streets taking a nap, I slipped out and hurried over to Joseph's house. I tapped on his wall three times. That was our little signal for him to "go out for a walk."

I guess you would think our betrothal customs were very strange. Being betrothed to someone was as binding a commitment as being married. It could only be broken by death or divorce. A woman could get stoned for getting intimate with another man, and people would scold you if they saw you even talking to your betrothed in a personal way. So we had to be discreet.

I was very happy our families had chosen Joseph and me for each other. He was a righteous man, but not stern and stiff like my father. He had a big heart and a warm smile for everyone, especially me! I could tell he was fond of me, like I was of him.

"Mary, what brings you out on such a hot afternoon?" Joseph asked.

"Have you had any unusual dreams lately, Joseph?" I asked.

He blushed a little in spite of himself. "Mary, I have to confess I have lots of dreams these days, I mean nights, well, and days too. And you're in every one! Now why are you asking me a question like that?"

"Oh, it's nothing," I said, biting my lip.

"Mary, what's the matter with you?" He motioned me to follow him behind his father's shop where we couldn't be seen, and got me to tell him everything.

"So what you're telling me is that you're pregnant. And you want me to believe that it wasn't a man that got you pregnant? It's the Most High, the Lord of heaven and earth, blessed be His holy name. Mary, what do you take me for? That never even happened to anyone in the Scriptures! Now Mary, I'm a man of character. At least give me the courtesy of telling me the truth! Please, Mary, tell me what happened!"

The anguish on his face was too much for me to bear. I closed my eyes, my whole body trembling. "It happened just the way I told you, Joseph."

I think the cry of agony that I heard came from his soul, not his mouth, because nobody came running from their homes. I opened my eyes and looked at his face. The light that once danced in his eyes when he looked at me was now a fierce burning coal.

"Go home, woman! I see that everything I believed about you was just a dream! I can't bear this! Now go home!" He ran into his house wringing his clothes.

"God!" I cried out loud as I ran back home. "What are you doing to me? What am I supposed to do? God, I'm just a girl! I just can't bear this alone!"

As I rounded the corner near my house, I felt a profound emptiness. My house was no longer a safe home. My mother thought I was mad. If I told my father, he wouldn't rest until "justice" was done—either Joseph would be punished or I would. I felt like I had no home, no family anymore.

Then I remembered. The angel had told me that my elderly cousin Elizabeth was pregnant, after all these years of being barren. Maybe she could believe in a miracle. I went into my house and told my parents I needed to go see Elizabeth.

"Whatever for?" my father demanded.

"I think we should let her go, Ezra." My mother almost looked relieved. "I think Mary needs a little change."

"But who will go with her?"

"God will go with me," I answered. I grabbed my other robe and a loaf of bread. I saw my mother hold his arm and pat his shoulder to restrain him as I headed out the door.

It was a two-day journey to Zechariah and Elizabeth's house. The determination I had felt leaving the house gave way to uncertainty as I wondered how to tell Elizabeth and Zechariah my news. They were very upright people. What if they sent me away as a disgrace to the family?

"Let it be with me according to your word," I had told the angel. Could I still trust God to be working some kind of good in all of this? Should I be like the old widow Sarah across the street, who was so beaten down by all her losses and poverty? She always says that whatever happens is God's will, and there's nothing you can do about it but suffer through it. Her heart seemed so closed. To her, God was almost her enemy, and she was His helpless victim.

"Let it be with me according to your word." Was I thinking like Widow Sarah when I said that to Gabriel? No. My heart had been open. I had trusted God's plan, that somehow it would be good. I didn't want to be a victim. I wanted to help God's plan happen. That's still what I wanted, to help give birth to God's plan, whatever it was.

"Let it be with me according to your word," I said out loud as I walked along. "Not as a helpless victim. I give You all of me, to work through as You see fit. Just don't abandon me, God. Please let me know You haven't left me to suffer alone!"

I finally arrived at Zechariah and Elizabeth's house, bracing myself for whatever happened next. When I went to the door and called Elizabeth's name, I heard a most unusual cry of surprise and joy. "Mary! Mary!" Her round belly came bouncing toward me, followed by her old frame. Her eyes sparkled with wonder. "God has blessed you more than any other woman! And God has blessed the baby which you will give birth to! You are the mother of my Lord, and you have come to me! Why has something so good happened to me? When I heard your voice, the baby inside me jumped with joy. You are blessed because you believed what the Lord said to you would really happen."

I fell into Elizabeth's open arms, crying and laughing at the same time. Such relief and joy welled up, I couldn't contain it. "My soul praises the Lord, and my spirit sings for joy because God is my Savior! I am not important, but God has shown His care for me, His servant girl." And I began dancing around and praying this ecstatic prayer. God hadn't left me alone! And God was using me to give birth to a wonderful new plan. He was bringing down the powerful from their thrones, and lifting up the lowly, starting with me, a humble young maiden!

The three months I stayed with Elizabeth and Zechariah went all too quickly. When it was almost time for Elizabeth to deliver, I heard a familiar voice at the door. It was Joseph! He was so out of breath I wondered if he had run the whole way!

"Mary! Mary! I had an unusual dream too!" he panted. "I saw your angel, Mary! He told me that everything you told me about your baby is true!" Joseph looked down at my little bulge with tender awe. "I'm so sorry I didn't believe you. The angel told me I should take you home with me as my wife, and be the baby's earthly father. Can we do that?"

"Let it be with me according to God's word!" I said, and I threw my arms around Joseph's neck. I didn't even care who saw us!

Well, I guess you know it wasn't "happily ever after" from then on. Giving birth to God's plan is seldom easy. When I was jostled on a donkey all the way from Nazareth to Bethlehem, about to deliver, I wondered why God would make us go to Bethlehem to have His baby. "Let it be with me according to your will," I kept praying, not yet knowing that we were fulfilling what the prophet had foretold.

When we couldn't even find a corner of a room at the inn, and had to rush to a stable as the labor pains came on hard, I wondered why God would allow His own Son to be born in a dirty place like that. "Let it be with me according to your will," I prayed between the pains, and with gasps and cries gave birth to the baby in a place even crude shepherds felt quite at home in. And you should have seen the wonder on those shepherds' faces when it began sinking in that God was including the likes of *them* in His new plan!

When Jesus was twelve, we were returning home from observing the Passover in Jerusalem. Joseph and I were desperate with worry when we couldn't find Jesus in our group of travelers. It took us three days of searching to finally find him back in the Temple. I wondered what kind of boy would dare to disregard us like that. When I scolded him, he calmly looked at us and said, "Why were you searching for me? Didn't you know that I need to be in my Father's house?"

"Let it be with me according to your will," I silently prayed, and I began to let Jesus follow a path that only he and his Spiritual Father could know.

Believe me, it was hard to keep from interfering when I saw him bringing more and more trouble on himself by preaching against our religious leaders. Then I had to watch him hanging on that blood-splattered Roman cross, his chest heaving as he gasped for each breath. I didn't know how to pray any more. I didn't want to pray. I was afraid that if I opened my mouth I would start cursing God for letting His plan come to such a hideous end.

I have to confess, it was only much later that I realized that Jesus' terrible death was the fulfilment of the new plan that God had started with me. God was emptying Himself, getting down so very low and vulnerable, and taking onto Himself even our haughty rejection of Him. The vulnerable, forgiving love He showed us opens the way for even the lowest of us to become God's own daughters and sons. That's what God was preparing to show us when He sent Gabriel to the home of a simple virgin and invited her to help Him with His marvelous new plan.

"Let it be with me according to your word." I am so glad I said that then. I am so glad I was able to say it at other very hard times along the way.

Do you know me any better now? Maybe you know yourself a little better now too. Haven't you struggled with hardships and trials you couldn't understand? Maybe not everything we endure happens for a higher purpose. But I know that some things do.

If we can keep our hearts open, and trust that God is with us, no matter how hard the going, even ordinary people like you and like me can help give birth to God's marvelous plan.

Soldier

"Quest for Power"

Luke 2:1-7

(The costume for this part should include a Roman soldier's helmet, which can be rented or purchased from a costume or party supply store. As an alternative, a sword may be used, with the sword being tossed onto the floor at the end instead of the helmet.)

Hail, subjects. Long live the Emperor! I'm Darius, a centurion officer in the mighty army of the Roman Empire. I served our great emperor Caesar Augustus in northern Judea. So when Caesar gave the decree that all of his subjects had to be registered for the Roman tax, I was ordered to oversee the enrollment in Bethlehem.

But I'm getting ahead of myself. Maybe you'd like to know something about me as a person. My father was a farmer. You would call him a peasant. He rented a little plot of dry, rocky land that we tried to get enough wheat from to keep some bread in our bellies. And, if we were lucky, maybe we could sell a little for things like some cloth to patch the holes in the rags that were supposed to cover our bodies. Farming was back-breaking work then—tilling that sun-baked soil with nothing but a crude hand plow, hauling water from the well in town to keep the plants from scorching in the sun, bending over from morning to night to plant the seeds or dig out the weeds or pick the grain.

But that way of life broke more than your back. It broke your spirit. I saw my parents' eyes get a little duller every time the crops failed, or another baby came along, or the landlord cursed our family and threatened to evict us when we couldn't pay our rent, or our oil jar broke when we had saved our precious pennies to dispel a little darkness. I could see my parents die a little more almost every day.

My people hadn't always been like this. Five hundred years before, Darius the Great had established the Persian Empire from Libya all the way to India. Giving me Darius' name was my father's way of keeping a little spark of pride alive in his soul. Long ago our people had some power. But the ruthless Parni tribe had defeated us two hundred years before, and robbed us of our land—and our pride.

Then, when I was just a boy, Caesar Augustus sent the mighty Roman army into our land which was known then as Parthia. Political infighting had weakened our rulers, and Rome quickly took control of our country. It didn't make that much difference to us peasants, except that now we were part of the Roman Empire and we were supposed to worship the Caesar who had defeated us like he was some kind of god.

When I was 17, some Roman soldiers came through our village to recruit young men into the Roman army. "Are you going to break your backs on this worthless soil for the rest of your lives?" they challenged. "Come and see places you can't even imagine! After twenty years, you'll be made a Roman citizen. If you stay here, in twenty years you'll be dead and buried in the ground you've killed yourself trying to work. Come with us and be a conqueror in the mightiest empire in the history of the world!"

When I got home, I couldn't shake their words out of my head. I looked at my father, powerless and broken. I got up my courage and talked to him about the soldiers.

"You want to join the *Roman* army? They defeated us just like the Parni, and now you want to join them? Remember your name, Darius. One day our people will find their strength again. Will you fight against us then?"

"Father, you've got to face reality. We're part of the Roman Empire now. What do you have to pass on to me? A worn-out plow, so I can break my back too? I can pass on to my children the rights of Roman citizenship, and a chance to be somebody in a new world I helped conquer."

My father didn't have the strength to argue with me, and all my mother could do was cry. And so I became a member of the mighty Roman army. I guess I showed leadership potential, because they eventually made me a centurion and put me in charge of the 100 or so men in our unit.

So that's how I came to be the officer who oversaw the registration for the Roman census in Bethlehem.

That doesn't sound like too hard a job. But the *hostility* I had to put up with made it a trial! I don't think any other people in the Roman Empire hated Rome as much as the Jews. Most people resigned themselves to the way things were. "When in Rome, do as the Romans do," was their philosophy. But the Jews believed that it was their God-ordained purpose to rule the world themselves. Can you imagine that?

They talked of a Messiah who was supposed to come and rule with supernatural power and put all their enemies under them like a footstool.

I hated the way those people looked at me. Behind the hatred, their eyes always had a smoldering spark of defiance. So we had to show them who had the power. When we were on the move, we'd catch Jewish men and make them carry our gear. If they cursed us or showed any kind of insolence, we'd beat them back down to their proper size.

But I couldn't help but feel a little sorry for the Jews. My people had once been a proud people too. Everybody wants to govern their own lives, and tell their children they can take pride in who they are, and give them some hope for a better future.

I sometimes thought about my father's parting words to me. "Remember your name, Darius. One day our people will find their strength again. Will you fight against us then?" What was this power I finally had hold of? Did it come from inner courage? From a commitment to a cause? From the strength of my convictions? Or was I just a powerless man who happened to be holding Caesar's sword?

Well, I didn't have time for such musings, because people were thronging into Bethlehem. Bethlehem, the little town that one of their prophets had said would produce a Messiah that would save the Jews from...well, from oppressors like me!

More Jews than I expected were claiming their greatest king, David, as their ancestor and coming to Bethlehem to register. I sent one of my men to Jerusalem for reinforcements, just in case this registration for the Roman tax in the City of David sparked a nationalistic rebellion.

I was glad to have those extra men with swords keeping an eye on things. I don't know how many angry complaints I heard about people's land being parched, and how the crops were sure to fail with the farmers gone to register for the tax. One man shook his fist at me while he told me he had to leave his dying father at home or face the soldiers' swords. Instead of beating him for his attitude, I thought about my family at home, and wondered how they would look as they came up to registration tables like this. Would *their* eyes have any spark of defiance, or would they just be bending a little lower and dying a little more?

I was afraid to picture the answer in my mind. But I was the one in power here. And everyone was coming to *me* with their complaints and requests.

"Where can I find some water? We're dying of thirst!"

"Isn't there any food to buy *anywhere*?"

"My son is terribly sick! You *have* to help me find a physician!"

All these people, all these plights, all these tears! Who was *I*, that *I* was supposed to solve every problem and meet every need? I had a helmet on, so they thought I had the power to help them. I had men with swords. I had a job to do. That's all I had.

"Get on now," I had to say. "I can't help you. Go on. Just finish the registration and go. *Out* with you, now!" Sometimes I had to reach for my sword before they'd listen.

There was one pair that really got to me, though. I saw the desperate, pleading look in the man's eyes as he talked to one of my men. He was talking fast with a Galilean accent, but he seemed to be saying his wife was about to have a baby and he needed to find shelter and a midwife. I looked over to where he was motioning, and saw her lying on the ground, so young—like my youngest sister—and so scared.

I stepped up to him. "Where are you from?" I demanded.

"Nazareth," he replied.

"Nazareth? That's got to be a week or two's journey! What in the name of Caesar did you bring *her* along with you for? You knew her condition!"

"I can't explain it all to you now, sir," he said. "But everyone thinks she was unfaithful to me, and that she should be stoned for adultery. I just couldn't leave her alone. Of course the Roman soldiers there wouldn't hear of any excuses, which I understand. Registering is a hardship for everybody. So here we are. I know you aren't in the baby business. I just don't know what to do, and she's already feeling her pains. Do you know *anywhere* we could go for shelter?" He searched my face as though he expected I might have an answer.

I shrugged my shoulders and looked away. "You can try the little inn down that street there," I said, and sent them off into the crowd. I knew full well there wasn't any room left in that flea-bitten place. But what else could I do?

I quickly walked away from the registration tables, away from the crowds, so I could sit by myself. I wore the helmet, the armor, and the sword of a soldier of the mighty Roman Empire. But where was my power? When it came down to things that used to seem so important, like the birth of a baby, or providing food and water to people, or keeping crops from dying, all my power did was disrupt and destroy. I felt just as powerless as that couple I had sent away.

We were locked into different roles for now. But we were equally powerless.

A strange thought hit me. I wonder if Caesar Augustus fights feeling powerless too? Maybe he feels locked in his role of the ruler of the mightiest empire in the history of the world, so he has to keep on conquering and taxing, or someone else will take all his power away from him. I started to chuckle out loud. "I'll bet our holy old emperor Caesar Augustus is afraid of losing control and feeling powerless just like the rest of us! Isn't it strange? Everybody thinks somebody else has the power. But nobody really does. *Everybody* is trapped in powerlessness, or trapped by the fear of it!

Well, that's the kind of thing I was thinking about while over in Bethlehem, the City of David, some strange kind of Messiah, some unexpected kind of Savior, was being born. See, everybody thought that their savior would be somebody with the biggest sword of all. If the Jewish army couldn't make a dent in Rome's armor, well then, God would send in angels working military miracles to take the power away from Rome, so the Jews could wield it.

But that's not what happened. Not at all! The baby who was born that day in the City of David grew up to tell the people, "If a soldier compels you to walk with him one mile, go with him two." "If someone strikes you on your cheek, turn to him the other one as well." "Love your enemies. Pray for those who persecute you."

If you're locked into your role of gaining power by taking it from someone else, then all of these things just sound like foolishness. But if you put down your sword and take off your armor and *really listen*, you'll begin to see that Jesus was offering *everybody* a way out of the powerlessness trap. He was saying, "If you get out of the role of the victim *and* the oppressor, you can begin to neutralize the power that destroys, and gain the power that builds."

I heard that he did that himself, even when our Roman soldiers spat on him, whipped him, and nailed him to a cross to die. He suffered, but not like a helpless victim, and not fighting back with hatred. And from what I've heard, his prayer asking God to forgive those soldiers because they didn't know what they were doing made them stop and *think* about what they were doing, and wish they weren't doing it. It's awfully hard to play the power game with someone who wants to build you with love's power, instead of taking your power away from you.

So today I take my helmet off to this man, who showed the world a kind of power a hundred Caesars could never see. *(He removes his helmet and tosses it on the floor.)* Has anyone else found it? Have you?

Innkeeper

"No Room"

Luke 1-7

What a lousy business I was in! I was the owner, bellhop, cook, and dishwasher of a small, run down inn in Bethlehem. You guessed it. I'm the innkeeper who turned away the mother and father of the Savior of the world, and put them in a cold, smelly stable. Little did I know that this one insignificant incident in the most harried time of my life would put me in the Bible, of all things! And believe me, folks, little did I know that this one little decision was going to force churches forever after to set up their nativity scenes to look like stables, with animals, feeding troughs, and straw that makes a mess on your nice carpets!

I've often wondered what would have happened if I had found a room inside for that couple. Would you set up the scene of a cheap hotel room in your church? See, we're not talking about a Holiday Inn here, or even a Motel 6. Oh, I would have liked to have run a nice place, like some of the inns in Jerusalem. But that was the problem. Jerusalem was only five miles away from Bethlehem. Bethlehem was just a no-account little town, with the wilderness at our back door. The rich merchants all stayed in Jerusalem. They came to Bethlehem to sell their goods, and take our money, but they never left any of it behind for us.

The guests at my inn were ordinary poor folks, sojourners (you would call them transients), shady characters, and Roman soldiers, who kept coming in as they traveled back and forth to Jerusalem, demanding free service. Can you believe that? It didn't matter to them that they were leaving me with nothing to feed my paying customers. It didn't matter to them that my wife and children and I had to go hungry after they raided our larder, or that I couldn't buy the materials to fix the leaky roof and the holes in the walls. It didn't matter to them that I was already supporting their bloody occupational forces with the tax money they extorted from me.

We couldn't keep going on this way. My children were looking thin, and their clothes were ragged. My poor wife, who worked herself to the bone to keep things running, couldn't hide the deepening lines of worry that were carved into her face. I hated the Romans! I hated poverty—my poverty and the sniveling poverty of my customers who always thought their three denarii should entitle them to better accommodations! I hated my lot as a powerless Jew in an unjust world where the Almighty God stayed nice and comfortable in heaven while His people suffered!

Do you blame me for that? Do you blame me for being a little bitter, when my family was going hungry?

Well, it so happened that I had an unexpected change in my luck. And it came from a most unexpected place. It came from the top Roman himself, Caesar Augustus, who sent out a decree that all the Roman world should be enrolled. Everyone had to enroll in their own home city. I guess they wanted to keep track of all the families together, and make sure nobody was slipping through the cracks and evading the Roman tax. Not too many Jews were rejoicing at this news. But when my wife and I heard it, we went dancing around our little room. There would be travelers coming to Bethlehem! There would be customers, plenty of customers! We could catch up at last, even get ahead of the game, and make a real profit for a change.

And it happened, just as we had hoped it would. People came from everywhere! I hadn't known so many people had moved out of Bethlehem, not that I could blame them. And by the looks of them, some of them had done pretty well for themselves. My wife and I made a plan. We would double, no, triple our prices for our rooms, and, if necessary squeeze more people in by putting mats on the floor. Why not? Now there were plenty of people who'd be willing to part with nine denarii to sleep in any kind of room!

Do you blame me for what I did? Do you blame me for seizing this once-in-a-lifetime opportunity to get my head above water and get ahead a little bit?

Well, our little inn was finally making some money. Of course people complained and even called us a few choice names when they heard our room rates. But what could they do? Sleep in the street? So they got back at us by making us really earn our money. "Innkeeper! Get me another blanket!" "Get me another drink!" "Fix this hole in my wall!"

We were working like dogs, day and night, trying our best to keep our customers satisfied. We were having one of those evenings when our most famous customers arrived—you know, the couple from Nazareth. Believe me, they sure didn't look famous when I saw them! Their clothes were plain and worn, and dirty from a long journey. The woman, or girl, really, was very pregnant, and her occasional gasping and grimacing made me suspect she wouldn't be much longer. These were not the kind of customers we were looking for! I told them, "Sorry, friends, but there isn't any room." And in fact, I was right. All of the beds were taken. There was still some floor space left, but how could I put a pregnant girl who was probably already in labor in a room with men? If I gave this couple a room of their own, I'd have to move everybody around, and put some good-paying customers who thought they had a bed on somebody else's floor. No way was I going to try that! Of course, there was the floor in my family's living quarters, but we didn't even know what sort of characters these people were. And my children didn't need to watch some girl hardly older than they were go through labor and delivery. I wasn't even sure this couple was married. "No," I said very firmly. "I just don't have any room for you in here."

Do you blame me for that? Do you blame me for not disrupting the whole inn and my family for this pair of strangers?

The couple just sort of stood there for a minute. I guess they didn't know where else to go. It was a shame what Caesar was putting people through, and I felt a little guilty for feeling so happy about this enrollment business. Some of my guests were shouting at me, "Innkeeper, where's my supper! Innkeeper!" I started to close the door. But the look on the girl's face made me hesitate. It was the same look of worry and desperate fear that had carved deep lines into my wife's face.

"Look," I said. "See that stable over there? For a denarius, you can use that, and give your donkey some hay. If you come in for meals, that's extra." The man paid me, and I went back to the business of taking care of my more important guests.

Well, that's how it happened. Was it my fault that Jesus Christ, the Son of God, was born in a stable, and laid in a feeding trough? Caesar's the one that should be blamed. Even so, I still feel kind of bad about the way it happened.

I've had lots of time to think about that strange night since then. I know now that God wasn't so far away as I thought during those dark times. I know now that God wasn't just letting this cruel world run its course, while He stayed all comfortable in His heavenly glory. I know now that on that very night, God came to us, right there in the middle of our oppression and suffering. He came to us, right there in the middle of our hatred and our greed too. They named that baby *Jesus,* which means "the Lord saves." They also called him Emmanuel, which means "God with us."

If I had known then what I know now, I would have done things differently. If Joseph and Mary knocked on my door, looking for a place to give birth to Jesus, I'd make room for them. You bet I would! Hey, I'd go sleep in the stable if I had to! I'm sure you would too, if you knew who it was.

But what I learned from that night was that God comes to us kind of sneaky, in ways we don't expect. If God came to me as another stranger, or as one who was hungry or thirsty, or cold, or sick, I wonder if I would have room then. If God came, not to make me rich, but to teach me how to give, I wonder if I would have room then. If God came, not to conquer my enemies, but to show me how to love them, I wonder if I would have room then.

This is the season you call Advent. Advent means "coming." What if God came to you this Advent, catching you by surprise as He knocked on your door to see if there's room for Him in your life? Would He find a life full of selfishness and bitterness, as He did with me? Would He find a life full of busyness and unimportant details to tend to, with no time for His people? This Advent, right now, is there room in your life for Emmanuel, "God-with-us," to be born?

Shepherd

"To Us"

Luke 2:8-20

I have been wanting to share with you what happened to me on that starry night so long ago. So I got up my courage, and here I am. I can't quite believe that no one has objected yet! See, I was a shepherd, and we weren't allowed to be in places of worship or to associate with righteous people. They called us unclean. Why? Because the Scribes and the Pharisees taught the people that in order to be acceptable to God, you had to go through all this ritual hand washing every time you turned around, and cook your food in certain ways, and obey lots of other little rules that we shepherds just couldn't do way out in the wilderness where we spent most of our time.

But you know something? I think the real reason people looked down on us is because they had gotten so citified, they just didn't like the way we smelled! So on the rare occasions when I ventured into town, I used the back streets and stayed away from the synagogue, and I tried not to let it bother me that people made funny faces when they caught wind of my rustic aroma.

As you can imagine, it was a pretty lonely life, being a shepherd. But my father was a shepherd, and his father before him. So I just accepted my lot in life, and spent day after lonely day wandering over the distant hills, trying to keep my flock of dumb sheep alive.

They are dumb, too. I don't think I ever met a sheep that had any sense. Sheep can't see any farther than what is right in front of them. They need a shepherd to find good grazing land for them, and even to show them where the water is. If one sheep starts heading for a cliff and acts like he knows what he is doing, the others just follow right along. Sheep are always getting hurt, or getting lost. And they have no way to defend themselves against the wolves and even lions that live in the wilderness. Without a good shepherd leading them, I don't think a flock of sheep would last two days out there.

I often thought about my people as being like a flock without a shepherd. I knew that my people worshiped a God who had supposedly chosen us to be His own special flock. He had rescued us from slavery in Egypt, and given us the Law and the prophets, so we could be a light to the nations. That's the way the story went. But now it seemed like God had just left His flock to fend for themselves. My people were lost. The Scribes and Pharisees acted like they knew what they were doing, so the people followed. But the place they led the people was more like brambles than green pastures. Instead of being fed, everyone was getting tangled up on the thorny points of the law. At least that's how it seemed to me. Why had God left us alone in the wilderness? And why had He let us fall prey to Rome, who had fallen on us like a lion traps its prey?

I guess it was at night that I thought about these things the most. As the last glow of the sun faded over the distant hills, I'd take out my shepherd's pipe and play quiet, lonely tunes to calm the sheep for the night. And then I'd watch the stars come out, first one here and there, and then pretty soon the whole vault of heaven would be sprayed with dots of light. I'd lie on my back and look up. I was just one tiny speck in a vast ocean of space. A fragment of a psalm I had heard as a child came to me. It was a Psalm of David, the shepherd. The part I remembered went:

> *"When I look at your heavens, the work of your fingers, the moon and the stars which you have established; what are people, that you are mindful of them, mortals, that you care for them?" (Psalm 8:3-4)*

Yes. That said it well. And who am I, one smelly, lonely no-account shepherd, that God would have any interest in me?

It was one of those brilliant nights that I wanted to tell you about. On that particular night, I wasn't alone. It was early in the year, and there was still good grazing in the hills close to Bethlehem. So four of us shepherds herded our flocks over to the same hill and gathered at the top to keep each other company. As the sun set, we took out our pipes and shared our favorite tunes with each other. Each man's tunes spoke of the loneliness he carried in his heart. Then we talked about our lives as shepherds. Was there any hope that life would ever yield any more for us than loneliness, shame, and the disgusted stares of the righteous people? No, we decided. Our fate was as set as the courses of the stars that were filling the sky overhead.

But that was a curious thing. There was a bright new star, directly over us, that we all had noticed on recent nights of star gazing. We all lay on our backs looking up at it, trying to figure out what it could mean. Was something new going to happen here below? That night, as we pondered the dazzling sky together, the heavens seemed to shimmer in pregnant mystery.

And then, as we lay there, I began to have the sense that we weren't alone. There was a presence there with us. And then it was as though that presence began to become visible in the form of a light, a light that was more radiant than any light we had ever seen. We all scrambled to our feet, wondering where to run for cover! But a voice spoke to us. I still don't know if I heard it through my ears or through my heart. It said, "Don't be afraid. Listen. I bring you good news of great joy which will come to all the people. For to you is born this day in the city of David, a Savior, who is Christ the Lord."

What was happening to us? Out of this immense vault of the heavens came a voice speaking to *us*, a bunch of smelly shepherds, "To you is born a Savior, the Messiah." Didn't this angel know who we were? I vaguely remembered hearing as a child that the prophet Micah had said that the Messiah would be born in Bethlehem. But that had been 700 years ago. If this prophecy was to be fulfilled after all this time, it surely wouldn't be a few lowly shepherds who would get the advance notice! We didn't know *what* was happening to us, but it couldn't be real.

The angel, or whatever it was, seemed to sense our disbelief. The voice spoke again, "This will be a sign for you: you will find a baby wrapped in swaddling cloths and lying in a manger." And then, I kid you not, it was like the whole sky burst into singing. It was beautiful voices filling the whole sky, singing praises to God.

The Bible says that we made haste to go to Bethlehem. That sounds so polite! We didn't just make haste, we ran out of there so fast our feet hardly touched the ground—less in eagerness to see a baby than in fear for what might happen next if we stuck around! But when we finally slowed to a walk close to town and caught our breath, we tried to make some kind of sense of what had just happened. The Messiah being born that day in Bethlehem...that part we could half believe. But lying in a manger, a dirty, smelly feeding trough? That's not what God would choose for a king, a mighty ruler who would come to judge the wicked and lead the righteous to victory over their enemies. And we all heard the angel say the same thing: "To you is born a Savior." He was speaking to *us*. None of this was making any sense!

We wandered around town a little, almost hoping we wouldn't find anything unusual, and we could dismiss the whole thing as some kind of a dream. But then we heard the cry of a baby. It seemed to be coming from behind that shabby old inn. We followed the sound to a stable. Even for us shepherds, the smell seemed pretty rank! Back in the corner were a frightened girl and a man eyeing us warily. And right between them was a manger, with a baby moving around and making baby noises! We just stood there with our mouths hanging open. "To you is born a Savior." Not to the wealthy, or the righteous, or the powerful. "To you," the angel had said, and he *had* meant us! Here was a baby, born in a smelly manger and the cold, to lonely parents who were shut out of the inn. Maybe *here* was a Savior who would know the suffering of his people! Maybe *here* was a Shepherd who would really know his sheep!

Without thinking, we fell to our knees in front of that helpless little baby. I felt like I should pray or do something holy, you know? But all I could do was weep. I thought I would never know anything but being rejected by people and forgotten by God. Why

God chose us nobodies to give His gift to, I couldn't explain. But here it was, just like the angel had said!

We tried to tell the young couple what had happened to us out on the hill. They didn't look at us like we were crazy. In fact, the frightened, defeated look on their faces gave way to a look of hope. Then they began talking real fast, about how angels had talked to them too. It was like we were the first ones who had ever believed them!

Before we left, we all stood around the manger, arms around each other in a holy circle of love and hope. We wondered what God had in mind for this child. Then the father's eyes lit up as he recalled a passage from the prophet Ezekiel:

> *"I myself will be the shepherd of my sheep, . . I will seek the lost, and I will bring back the strayed, and I will bind up the crippled, and I will strengthen the weak,...and I will feed them in justice" (Ezek. 34:15-16).*

As we shepherds made our way back out to the hill, our feet hardly touched the ground again. But this time it was because we were almost floating. Our eyes were transfixed by the brilliant stars, which seemed to dance around the new star in the sky. Suddenly, the rest of that Psalm of David came back to me:

> *O Lord, our Lord, how majestic is your name in all the earth!*
>
> *You whose glory above the heavens is chanted by the mouth of babes and infants, you have founded a bulwark because of your foes, to still the enemy and the avenger.*
>
> *When I look at your heavens, the work of your fingers, the moon and the stars*

which you have established; what are people, that you are mindful of them, mortals, that you care for them?

Yet you have made them a little less than God, and crowned them, with glory and honor....

O Lord, our Lord, how majestic is your name in all the earth!

(Psalm 8)

Wise Man

"Follow that Star"

Matthew 2:1-12

Do you know what it's like to try to explain something that's very important to you to the people who are closest to you, and see them shake their heads and walk away? Or worse yet, you hear them whispering how worried they are about you!

That's what happened to me when I told my own people that I was going to travel to Judea to look for the baby whose birth was announced by the star. I know *you* don't think I'm crazy, because, after all, we found the child you worship as your Savior. But it sure would be reasonable to wonder how a star could make anyone travel hundreds of treacherous miles without any idea of who they were looking for, or any guarantee they'd find anything at all. It does sound a little, what's your expression, nuts, doesn't it?

So how can I help you understand why we made that journey? I could tell you that throughout the whole civilized world of 2000 years ago, people shared a pessimism about humanity's ability to govern itself with any kind of peace or justice or respect for higher values than money and power. In the West, the "Pax Romana," the era of world order and peace that was supposed to be brought by the great Roman Empire, had grown sour with all the infighting and oppression by the small-minded Roman rulers.

In the East, where I lived, the Persian Empire had fallen into the same kind of abuse of power. My ancestry goes back to the Medes. We were a highly cultured people who had been conquered by the power-hungry Persians. Once my people had tried to overthrow the Persian rulers, but we were overpowered by Persia's military strength. After that, we had to resort to trying to influence the people in power by using our highly developed wisdom and knowledge. Many of the men in my tribe became known as the magi, the wise men, and we were the teachers, scientists, and advisors of our day. We weren't kings, but some of us were advisors to kings. The Roman statesman Cicero once wrote, "No Persian is able to become king who has not first mastered the scientific discipline of the Magi."[1]

I happened to be an advisor to a Persian lord, Jahara. I had a position that should have enabled me to elevate our kingdom to a higher moral level. So often I dreamed of what our kingdom would be like if it were truly governed on the basis of the highest human wisdom and principles available. But Lord Jahara reduced all my advice to the simple question: What would best protect his power and advance his position?

Throughout the world it seemed to be the same. Armies and nations clashed and rose and fell; the people suffered from wars, abuse and oppression; truth and wisdom were trampled under the horses and chariots of those in power. People of all religions wondered: Would God, or the gods, ever bring to this earth another way?

I could also tell you that there was a general feeling in much of the world that a great leader would come from Judea, the land of the Jews. The ancient Roman historian Seutonius wrote, "There had spread over all the Orient the old and established belief, that it was fated at that time for men coming from Judea to rule the world."[2]

So you see, there were some vague feelings of expectation and hope in the air, especially directed toward Judea. But they don't begin to explain why I and two other magi left behind the comfort and security of homes and set off for a faraway land.

For that, I guess you have to know more about me. Like most magi, I was fascinated by the stars. Now think for a minute about what the world was like in my day. We had diseases, famines, earthquakes and wars, all keeping us in turmoil. Then look up and think about the starry heavens, home of the gods. At first a starry sky looks like a jumble of chaos too. But study it. You begin to see that the stars are formed into certain patterns that appear night after night. The more you study, the more order you see. The constellations move in regular patterns. The planets, the sun, and the moon have their own regular courses. You can even predict eclipses, which really impresses your friends!

Now, put the two realms together, the earth and the heavens. What if the forces that govern the motions of the stars also govern the events of the earth? It governs seasons, the crops, animals; the cycles of the moon even govern women's fertility. Our penetrating minds searched for and studied less obvious connections between the heavens and the earth—cycles of rain and drought, the rise and fall of kings, fortune and misfortune. We developed an elaborate system for predicting lots of things.

This was my quest, you see, to be able to penetrate the appearance of things to understand the underlying principles. If you understand how nature's processes work, and how things are likely to turn out, well, then you begin to gain mastery over it. That's why Lord Jahara took good care of me. I told him when it would be fortuitous to go to battle, and when to be cautious. I told him when hidden danger threatened, and when luck would be on his side. That was my job, at least that's what he demanded of me; and he was the master. It seemed to be my destiny to prostitute my knowledge and wisdom to his lust for power.

Anyway, you can imagine our fascination when a brilliant conjunction of Saturn and Jupiter appeared in the sky, outshining anything of its kind we had ever seen. What did it mean? We magi had all kinds of ideas, but we had to wait two years to find the answer. For the next three years, on the first day of the month called Mesori, the star Sirius rose at sunrise and shone with extraordinary brilliance. Now the name Mesori means "the birth of a prince," and such a bright star, preceded by the convergence of two planets, told us of a very important birth.

Now we had to figure out where this great prince might be born, for no prince had been born to our king. One of the magi found this prophecy in the Jewish holy writings: "A star shall rise out of Jacob." Jacob was one of the Jewish patriarchs. These strange events in the sky seemed to announce the birth of a very important leader coming from the Jews, just like people were mysteriously expecting.

I told Lord Jahara about the star, and about what I knew about the history of the Jews. Their nationhood had been born when God had called Moses to lead his people out of slavery in Egypt. And with

God's help, this disorganized, unarmed band of slaves had escaped from Egypt, organized their society around a strong moral and religious law, and become a strong people. What would this *new* leader of the Jews do, we wondered together? "Well, he'll probably give the Romans a rough go of it. And that can't be bad for us, now, can it? Unless the Jews become as strong as the Romans!" He went into fits of laughter at that preposterous idea. "Now, Melchior, what do the stars say about my luck today? Can I sack that judge who let Arzan go free, when three witnesses heard him criticize my new tax? They should both be beheaded for insubordination! What do the stars say about *that,* Melchior?"

"I don't see anything in the stars that would specifically forbid it, but doesn't that seem a bit harsh?"

"I'll describe what's harsh, you tell me what the stars say, Melchior." New star or not, it was business as usual in our kingdom.

But it wasn't business as usual for me. I couldn't get that star out of my mind. Every night it appeared in my dreams, shining bigger and brighter than everything else. It seemed to be trying to draw me to follow it to heed its call, to find the prince whose birth it was announcing to us. But I had no idea why.

How many hours did I spend in the dark, wrestling with what this dream meant? Should I offer to go as an emissary from Persia? I didn't know anything about making political treaties and deals. And besides, Lord Jahara would be the first to point out that you don't make deals with babies, especially when they're under Roman rule.

I quietly confided in a few close magi friends. All they did was raise the same doubts and questions I had asked myself a hundred times already: the journey to Judea would take months, and it was very difficult and dangerous. How would I know where to go once I got there? What would I do if I found the prince? What would happen to my family while I was gone—and if I never came back? "I know, I know," was all I could say. But the star would not be silenced by good sense.

My wife begged me to tell her why my nights had been so restless and my waking so distracted. When I told her, a look of deep worry shaped her face, a look that never left her, and she watched my every move out of the corner of her eye after that. That's when the head-shaking and the worried whispers started, and I will tell you that I doubted my own sanity as much as any of them. I hated that infernal star!

But it wasn't that simple. Part of me couldn't hate it. How could I sustain hate for the only thing that shone light into a life that was so clouded with forces of darkness? How could I hate the one thing that held out hope for a new kind of government, one that God was calling me to learn?

I had a choice to make—the most important one in my life. Would I stay with the things I could figure out and make sense of and master? Or would I say "yes" to something that I might never be able to explain or master at all, but that somehow might make sense to me as I let it be *my* master? Would I stay within the security of a compromised magi in a corrupted world? Or would I say "yes" to something that would draw me out of my security, yet bring me closer to a peace that I sensed was greater than any peace I had found in the safety of cowardice. I would have to leave so much behind if I said "yes" to the star.

I don't know if I would have dared to say "yes," if friends hadn't begun telling me of two other magi in other courts who had been talking about the star like I was. When we first met each other, each of us was relieved that we weren't crazy after all. Then we were afraid to death that we weren't crazy after all, because we were going to have to follow that star!

I could tell you so many stories about our journey! It took most of one year just to get there, and we encountered storms, bandits, water shortages, and sickness. We learned that being faithful to your call doesn't make things easy. The journey was hard. We had to use Herod to locate the child, but outwit him to avoid falling into his trap. We learned the importance of shrewdness, resourcefulness, and flexibility as we doggedly followed that star.

When we finally found the Prince we had been searching for, we were quite surprised. He didn't look like a prince at all! Instead of the trappings of wealth and power, we found a humble home of simple faith in God and love for each other, and very gracious hospitality for us very strange-looking foreigners. But we had no doubts that we had found the baby we were looking for. The warmth and love that we experienced there, and the hope that Joseph and Mary shared with us as they told us their amazing story, made us glow with the same gently radiating light that had touched us in our dreams.

In this small room in Bethlehem, with a poor young couple and their little baby, we had mysteriously come home. It was like we were all one family, linked by a Source of Light and Love, Peace and Truth that was beyond all understanding. But it was the most real thing I had ever experienced. I would have made the journey a thousand times just to be so close to that wonderful light, and to let it fill me so.

What I learned is that it is worth everything to follow that star, to trust its wisdom that is far higher than our own, and to let it lead you home, however far, or however close, home may be. That trip to Bethlehem was really just the beginning of the journey for me, and the other magi too. The hardest part was the part that awaited us after we returned home, when we tried to live in faithfulness to the wisdom that the star had given us. But you know something? With the birth of that Prince of Peace, a new way of governing human affairs *was* born, even in our kingdom in Persia. Oh, historians probably wouldn't have noticed it. But our families did, and our friends, and our lords. Jahara didn't always like it. Standing my ground and advising him out of the best wisdom in me sometimes got me in trouble. But we were never abandoned by our hope that the glow of that light would keep shining in us, and maybe even through us.

Well, that's the best way I know how to tell you how I happened to travel to Bethlehem 2000 years ago. Does it make any sense to you? Is it possible you might have done something like that too? Is it possible you already have? Are you already on a journey of faith and hope? Has something led you to choose faith over mastery, peace over security? I hope so. I'd like nothing more than to have you as traveling companions, so that together we can follow the light of that Prince's star.

[1]Interpreter's Dictionary of the Bible. Vol. 3. New York, NY: Abingdon Press, 1962. p. 222.

[2]Barclay's Daily Study Bible. Vol. 1. Philadelphia: The Westminster Press, 1958. p. 18.

Herod

"Two Paths to Peace"

Matthew 2:13-18

My name is Herod the Great. Yes, I'm the ruler of the Jews who gave the order to kill all the male babies in Bethlehem. You probably think that I must have been an incredibly evil, twisted man to do such a thing. Well, I can't deny that I wish now I hadn't done it. The blood of those innocent babies is on my hands, and the screams of their heartbroken mothers will ring in my ears for eternity. But, I will not let you make me out as some abnormal, sub-human maniac whose heart was made of stone. Oh no. My feelings and motives were as normal as the people you see every day. As you listen to my story, I'll let you be the judge of how different I am from them—and you.

You probably don't know this, but I did a lot of good things in my day. As just one example, I planned and constructed the beautiful city of Caesarea Maritima, which was very advanced in its day. We used enormous blocks of stone to create a harbor. We designed a sewage system that was flushed by the sea. And, here's something that will surprise you. I was the one who began the 84-year project of rebuilding the magnificent Jewish Temple in Jerusalem that you read so much about in your New Testament.

You see, I wanted to make a lasting contribution to civilization. I hoped that when I was old, I would be able to look around at the world I had walked on and see my indelible mark there. I wanted to be able to say, "Well done, Herod. You will be remembered for this."

Is that so bad a motive? Don't you want that too, to look back on the work you have completed, or the family you have raised, or the church you have given to, and say, "Well done. Well done. You have made your contribution. You will be remembered for what you have accomplished." Is that so bad?

The trouble is, there are people out there who want to take away your power so *they* can control things. You've known people who are all friendly to you, but as soon as they have your trust, they try to manipulate you or use you in some way. You've known people who try to control you by intimidation and fear. They keep all the power in their hands by keeping you dependent on their approval and afraid of their punishment. I'll bet you parents have used that tactic sometimes on your own children. And I'll bet that your children have returned the favor by manipulating you, taking advantage of you, getting you to wait on them, taking from you as much of your parental authority as they could get away with. You know what I'm talking about. This kind of thing happens all the time.

Well, in my position, there were plenty of people around who wanted to rob me of my power. I felt like those wild dogs were nipping at my ankles from every direction. First it was a bunch of thugs that was trying to take control of Galilee. I put them down. Then it was the Hasmoneans, the family that ruled the Province of Judea until Rome gave me the throne and made me the king of the Jews. Those

Hasmoneans gave me no end of trouble. I even took a Hasmonean as one of my wives to make peace and neutralize my opposition. But wouldn't you know it? My own wife turned traitor on me, and got three of my own sons to join her family in plotting against me. What was I to do? Just surrender to these murderous traitors? I had no choice. I had them executed: my wife, her family, and even my own sons. It was the hardest thing I ever did. But they had willfully tried to destroy me. If I hadn't eliminated them, they would have eliminated me.

But even that swift and sure justice didn't stop the plots. The people in Judea kept trying to mount revolts. They were a stiff-necked people, and I met them on their own terms.

Well, while all of this was going on, those three magi from the East came looking for the one who was born king of the Jews. They said they had seen his star, and wanted to pay homage to him. Now even the stars in the heavens seemed to be plotting against me and naming someone else for my position! That did it! I wasn't going to tolerate any more subversion, no matter where it came from. So I sent the magi on their way with clear orders to tell me where they found the child, "so that I too could go and worship him," I said. Well, they tricked me back and went home by another way, so I couldn't find him.

But I wasn't going to let their deception jeopardize my future! My throne belonged to me and my family, not some unknown baby! Since I couldn't find out which baby the star had shone for, all the possible candidates would have to be eliminated. It was another hard choice. But I had lost all patience with these evil forces who were threatening to undo me. I had to purge my kingdom of subversion, no matter what the cost!

So you see, I had become a man possessed by fear. I didn't set out to destroy or kill. All I had wanted was the power to create and build noble things. But as I look back on what happened, I realize now that I stopped using my power to build. More and more, my power became the servant of my fear; and my fear proved to be a very destructive master. Because of my fear, I was blinded to the humanity of the people I was afraid of. So I destroyed them.

Was I an unusually evil person, whose crimes were subhuman? May I ask you a personal question? Do you know what it feels like to just want to let your anger loose and really hurt someone, even the people that are closest to you, that you live with and work with all the time? I'm sure you haven't resorted to execution, like I did. But haven't you ever "lashed out" at someone with your tongue, so that they felt like they were given a lashing? Haven't you ever shot someone an angry look, so that they felt shot at? Haven't you ever tried to hurt someone with shame, hoping it would burn them like fire? Haven't you ever ridiculed someone, hoping your words cut like barbs?

Ah, yes, maybe you are beginning to see that I'm not as different from you as you thought. We are all just human, aren't we? I was afraid of having my position of influence, and my very life, stripped from me. What are the fears that take possession of your mind and begin controlling you? Does your fear of losing your parental authority over your kids ever drive you to dominate them as though they were your enemy? Does your fear of not being loved by your spouse drive you to nag, punish or manipulate, so that you destroy the love you are angry for not getting? Does your fear of being undercut or surpassed on the job keep you hostile, mistrustful, and anxious, creating the kind of atmosphere that's most likely to generate conflict against you? Does your fear of foreign competition drive you to vote for "America First" politicians who would further splinter the globe into isolated nations instead of a community of nations who can address common problems together?

Fear blinds us to the humanity of the people we are afraid of, and so we lose our ability to understand them and work with them. It was fear that drove me to kill my wife and my own sons. And it was fear that drove me to have all the male babies under two years old put to death.

I wonder if I would have reacted differently if those magi had referred to this baby by some other title than "king of the Jews." If they had said they were searching for one known to be the Prince of Peace, maybe my curiosity would have been aroused by that name, instead of my fear.

Because, you see, it was peace that I craved. Can you see the truth of that, in spite of all the violent things I did? I just wanted peace, so I could accomplish the worthy goals I had set for myself. I just didn't know how to make peace happen.

But this Prince of Peace of yours tried to show you the path to peace. If I understand him right, he tried to tame the fears that we all carry deep inside us, by replacing fear with faith. He tried to show you that there is nothing in life, or in death, or in all creation, that can separate you from God's love. Everything that we are driven to protect at any cost, will pass away. How well I know that now! And everything you are afraid of will pass away too. But the one thing that does not pass away is God's love. As kingdoms and powers come and go, the one thing that can grow through all time is God's kingdom, which expands when people act in faith, not fear, and work together in respect, not mistrust. Doesn't that put our fears, real as they are, in a different perspective? The Prince of Peace came to show you that peace happens, not by the force of your control over other people, but by the force of God's love guiding your mind and your actions.

I wish I had known then what I know now. Because I never found the path to peace in my life on earth, I am tormented now by all of the violence I committed. But it's not too late for you. You still have time to find the path to peace. You still have time to open your eyes to each other, to see what precious gifts you are to each other, to understand your differences and build bridges of caring, to tear down the walls of mistrust, and to begin building the Kingdom of love that Jesus died to show you. I missed my chance, and I missed out on the only thing that was of eternal importance—the peace of God. Please, don't miss your chance!